Pastorale

Pastorale

A Collection of Lyrics by

Rod McKuen

Color photographs by
WAYNE MASSIE

STANYAN BOOKS

RANDOM HOUSE

A Stanyan Book
Published by Stanyan Books,
8721 Sunset Blvd., Suite C
Hollywood, California 90069,
and by Random House, Inc.
201 East 50th Street,
New York, N.Y. 10022
Printed in U.S.A.

Library of Congress Catalog
Card Number: 75-160062

Designed by Hy Fujita
Color photography: Wayne Massie
Black & white photos: David Nutter

Green pastures—for
my mother

CONTENTS

13 I Think Of You

16 When Am I Ever Going Home?

18 Fields Of Wonder

20 Three

22 Love Let Me Not Hunger

28 I'll Fly Northward

30 The Single Man

34 The Green Hills Of England

37 Before The Monkeys Came

40 Kill The Wind

43 Silver Apples Of The Moon

46 I've Saved The Summer

49 Moving Day

53 The Wind Of Change

I Think of You

When I'm alone at night
and there's no one to comfort me
I think of you.
And suddenly my pillow
is your face and arms.

And when the winter wind
comes chasin' after me
I think of you.
And it's as though
I crawled beneath a blanket,
soft and warm.

How did I get from dark to daylight
before you happened to pass by?
How did I find my way thru life
before you brightened up my sky?
Was there a sky at all
until you painted it for me?

How did I get on
'til you came along?

Who knows how many times
I pause in every day
to think of you?
As often as the sun sails out
upon the silent sea.

And if you're wondering
why it is I only think of you —
Well, it's because
I'd like to be as close to you
as you've become to me.

I think of you, I think of you.

When Am I Ever Going Home?

When am I ever going home
back to the fields
that I once knew
before I went to seek out
skies of bluer blue?

Oh, when will I leave London town,
when will my travelling
be through
why is it now the newness
seems no longer new?

Some spring or fall
if time is good to me
I'll ride away
in the arms of love
and come back home to me.

Now as the clock of youth unwinds,
old memories
overflow my mind
and I wonder when I'm all alone
when am I ever going home?

Fields of Wonder

Come and take my hand.
We'll go over yonder.
Together we can walk
the fields of wonder.

Stay with me a while
out beyond the summer.
Together we can run
the fields of wonder.

There's so much
I don't yet understand
the how and why of growing.
Maybe if you take me by the hand
we'll have an easier time
of learning, and knowing.

Let's go see the sun
before it stops its turning.
Together we can lie
in fields of wonder.

Lie down by my side
from here until forever.
Together we can stay
in fields of wonder—
And all the fields we find
are fields of wonder.

three

We were three,
my true friend,
my new love
and me.
None were happy as we
as we walked beside
the Mediterranean sea.

Passion grew, as passion has a will
and want to do.
And long before
the summertime was through,
they walked beside
the oceanside as two.

July's done,
it fell beneath
the knife of August sun
and out here where
the lonely pipers run
I walk beside
the oceanside,
as one.

Love, Let Me Not Hunger

The bumblebee goes
from the rose
to the marigold,
then goes back to the rose.
The caterpillar climbs
each ribbon of vine
even the caterpillar knows,
the day's so warm
you wouldn't dare touch it
if it lay down by your side.
So come to me, come to me,
my arms are open wide.

Love let me not hunger—
I've been alone so long.
How can a little taste
of wine be wrong?
We'll not get any younger.
Come listen to my song
and if you've had a hunger
perhaps you'll sing along.

The day's so warm
you can feel the sun.
What does it matter
what's done in the day
after the day is done?

Love let me not hunger.
Come and take my hand,
and if you've ever hungered
I know you'll understand.

I'll fly Northward

I'll fly northward
go there with the birds
where I can't be hurt
by smiles or even words.
I'll fly on strange wings
as lovers often do,
I'll fly northward
fly away from you.

I'll fly toward
the dark and distant hill
beyond the edge of everything
where nothing is the only thing,
the only void to fill.

I'll fly northward
following the sea
where I won't have to trust
in anyone but me.
I'll fly beyond the reach
of anything that's new,
I'll fly northward
fly away from you.

For Marian Segal

The Single Man

I live alone.
That hasn't always been
easy to do,
for just a single man.
Sometimes at night,
the walls talk back to me.
They seem to say
wasn't yesterday
a better day?

Always alone
at home or in a crowd,
the single man
off on his private cloud
caught in a world
that few men understand,
I am what I am,
the single man.

Once was a time
(I can't remember when)
the house was filled with love,
but then again
it might have been
imagination's plan
to help along
the single man.

The Green Hills of England

As a man with a window
opened on the world
I've made my way, stumbling,
but turning with the the turns
and with no ties to bind me
I've come here on my own,
My only friend my pocket,
my heart my only home.

And are the green hills of England
waiting still?
Beneath the same blue sky,
above the same gray sea?
The green hills of England
like a woman not yet loved
lying there, waiting,
in the morning.

Having been to the far fields
each meadow and each lea
now I've started wondering
what's left for me to see.
Are there frontiers uncharted,
towns as yet unknown
before I turn to find the path
leading me back home?

And are the green hills of England
waiting still?
Beneath the same blue sky,
above the same gray sea?
The green hills of England
like a woman not yet loved
lying there, waiting,
in the morning.

Though I eye every highway
and listen for the trains
and amble down the alleyways
even when it rains,
I'm aware of the need to be
more than on my own.
I could dance down the distance
if the hills led me back home.

And are those green hills of England
waiting still?
Beneath the same gray sky,
Above the same blue sea?
The green hills of England
like a woman needing love,
lying there, waiting,
in the evening.

Even with so many worlds
left in life to see
the green hills of England
keep on pulling me.

For Stewart Morris

Before the Monkeys Came

We'll go wild into the noon
to find what love there is to find,
an angel on the bedpost
or a demon in the mind.
And we'll be happy as we were
before the monkeys came
and put the flowers into pots
and gave love sinful names.

When apple trees were apple trees
and not the curse of man
and all the mountains piled high
were only heaps of sand.
There were no yellow roses then,
the roses all were red,
and lovers slept on grassy banks
and never knew a bed.

We'll go wild into the noon
to find what love there is to find,
an angel on the bedpost
or a demon in the mind.
And we'll be happy as we were
before the monkeys came
and put the flowers into pots
and gave love sinful names.

Kill the Wind

They've not yet found a way
to kill the wind,
but they will.
As sure as they
trod down to dust
the poppies on the hill.
As sure as they
can burn the growing grass,
don't ask if they
can kill the wind.

They've not yet found a way
to harness time
but they will,
as sure as they
have shot the crow
and killed the whippoorwill.
As sure as they
have muddied up the stream,
it would seem
they'll learn to
kill the wind.

As on distant battlefields
young men fall again
thank God, at least
they've not yet found
a way to kill the wind.

The Silver Apples
of the Moon

Sometimes I find myself thinkin'
man really hasn't got a lot.
Still, for who he is
and where he's at,
does he deserve the world he's got?
The silver apples of the moon,
the golden apples of the sun.
The golden apples of the sun,
the silver apples of the moon.

It happens early in the morning
when I go walking on the beach.
The moon hangs low enough
to touch with a ladder;
still it's always out of reach.

The silver apples of the moon,
the golden apples of the sun.
The golden apples of the sun,
the silver apples of the moon.

And men still climb the stars
and men still chart the seas
and even love is getting better,
people easier to please.

Tomorrow is the wine of wonder
it teaches all there is to teach
and if we're patient
and we talk to one another
there'll soon be nothing
we can't reach.
The silver apples of the moon
the golden apples of the sun.
The golden apples of the sun,
the silver apples of the moon.

I've Saved the Summer

I've saved the summer
and I give it all to you
to hold on winter mornings
when the snow is new.

I've saved some sunlight
if you should ever need
a place away from darkness
where your mind can feed.

And for myself I've kept your smile
when you were but nineteen,
till you're older you'll not know
what brave young smiles can mean.

I know no answers
to help you on your way,
the answers lie somewhere
at the bottom of the day.

But if you've a need for love
I'll give you all I own
it might help you down the road
till you've found your own.

 Moving Day

I took down all the boxes
from the attic.
It was hard to throw
the old letters away,
but somehow the pages
had turned yellow
and it was time I had
another moving day.

I called up the Salvation Army,
told them come and take
my old life away.
Forgotten and faded are
the pictures in the hallway
and it's time I had
another moving day.

This little house has kept
the two of us together
so much together we're apart
and I guess the only thing
I really regret
is not finishing the lives
we tried to start.

I found that old coat
that's been missing,
the one I thought
you'd given away.
Now the only thing
that's missing is tomorrow;
but I'll find that
on another moving day.

It's a moving day.

The Wind of Change

Quietly
like the breeze
that blows the olive tree
the wind of change
has come down
from the hills
to lead me home again
through the last mile of sunshine.

As easily
as the moon makes patterns
on the lifeless lake
man grinds the flowers
of the fields beneath his heels
and you wonder if he feels
love, or even boredom,
and my friend—
the wind of change
is asking questions.

Suddenly
there are now
so many giants everywhere
so many men who think
even God looks small
when they're walking tall
and the wind of change is troubled.

Could it be
that he smiles because
he's seen this all before
and he knows the world
is finally going back to dust
and if we trust those men
who trample on the grass
emptiness is all that we
can hope to ask for.

Listen and hear
the sound of
the dying grass bleed
it's bleeding for man
and the poor fool
just won't understand,
and it's too late to change
the wind of change.

For Petula Clark

ABOUT THE AUTHOR

Rod McKuen was born in Oakland, California and grew up in California, Nevada, Washington and Oregon. He has traveled extensively both as a concert artist and as a writer. In the past three years his books of poetry have sold in excess of five million copies in hardcover, making him not only the best-selling poet of this age but probably every other era as well. In addition, he is the composer of more than a thousand popular songs. His film scores include The Prime of Miss Jean Brodie, A Boy Named Charlie Brown (both of which earned him Academy Award nominations), Scandalous John, Joanna and, with Henry Mancini, Me Natalie.

His major classical works, Symphony No. 1, Concerto No. 1 For Four Harpsichords and Orchestra, and Concerto for Guitar and Orchestra, have been performed by leading American symphony orchestras as well as those in foreign capitals of the world.

Before becoming a best-selling author and composer, Mr. McKuen worked as a laborer, radio disc jockey, newspaper columnist and as a psychological warfare script writer during the Korean War.

When not traveling, he lives at home in California in a rambling Spanish house with three sheep dogs and a menagerie of cats.